SATIN AND SILK
RIBBON EMBROIDERY

LESLEY TURPIN-DELPORT

First published 1993.
Second impression March 1994
Third impression March 1995
Fourth impression December 1995

ISBN 0-620-17755-1   Hard Cover Edition
ISBN 0-620-17756-x   Soft Cover Edition

PUBLISHED BY

Triple T Publishing
29 Colenso Road
Claremont 7700
Cape Town, South Africa.

NORTH AMERICAN DISTRIBUTORS

Quilters Resource Inc.
P.O. Box 148850
Chicago IL 60614
U.S.A.

Other books published by Triple T Publishing
JUST FLOWERS by Lesley Turpin-Delport ISBN 0-958-38733-8
TWO CUSHIONS AND A QUILT by Sue Akerman ISBN 0-958-38731-1
THE LIBERATED CANVAS by Penny Cornell ISBN 0-958-38734-6

Typesetting and reproduction by Fotoplate, Cape Town
Printed by Mills Litho, Cape Town
Text, illustrations and photographs by Lesley Turpin-Delport
Photographs on pages 4 & 5 and the back cover by Roger Wooldridge

The folded rosebud technique described on page 21 was taught by Elly Sienkiewicz in her book
Baltimore Beauties & Beyond, Studies in Classic Album Quilt Applique, Volume I
(1989 C&T Publishing, Martinez, CA 94553. USA) The method for ruching (page, 21)
is also illustrated in the same book.
Both methods are shared here with Elly's permission.

Photographs on:

Front Cover – detail of Valentine Heart.
Notice the interesting dimensions possible with satin and silk
ribbon in combination with crewel embroidery. *(Susan Sittig)*

Back Cover and Project page 25
A soft lawn handkerchief is embellished with gentle colours in
a profusion of different flowers. *(Robyn Rebe)*

Title page
Scatter cushions add charm to a garden bench. The ecru doilies
are cleverly worked with ribbon flowers and a few pearls.
(Annelie van Rensburg)

Pages 4 & 5
A hand-dyed, turn of century handkerchief is embellished with
satin and silk in a most unusual colour combination, inspired by
the rust-coloured background. *(Susan Sittig)*

Special Acknowledgements

*Very special thanks to my fabulous pupils, needlecraft friends and franchise teachers for all their help
and support during this production.*

*Dedicated to
JESS.*

INTRODUCTION

My love affair with embroidery began when I embellished appliqued moths and butterflies with free-style crewel stitches.

I have constantly experimented with composite stitches and 3-dimensional effects for form and texture. Imagine my delight when I stumbled upon the antique techniques of ribbon embroidery!

The author at home.

Here we have texture, 3rd dimension and an amazingly quick hand embroidered effect. I have combined satin and silk ribbon embroidery in this book as they are so complimentary to one another. Yet I have also handled the techniques in separate chapters to make it a little easier for the reader.

The essential difference between silk ribbon embroidery and satin is that the silk is so soft that it can be pulled through the background fabric just like embroidery floss. Simple crewel stitches work best and of course, I have included a few trick combinations. Silk ribbon is available in 2, 3.5 and 7mm. I prefer the 3.5mm as it is the most versatile of the three widths. My choice of background fabric is any natural fibre; silk, cotton, lawn, linen or wool. Rayon ribbon, when available, works well using the silk ribbon technique.

Satin ribbon is best manipulated and worked off the background fabric. Construct leaves and flowers as free-form shapes, then work the petals onto the background using invisible hemming stitches.

Satin ribbon can be softened with touches of crewel embroidery and silk foliage. Fine satin ribbon does pull through open weave fabrics such as evenweave or coarse linen and wool. The free-form methods described in Chapter 2 (page 17) dealing with satin ribbon also work well with 7mm silk ribbon.

I love combining different media, and feel you should experiment with the techniques and basic stitches described, using a wide range of ribbons such as silk, rayon, satin or velvet. I have included a glossary of crewel stich combinations which I really enjoy and would like you, the reader, to play with these stitches and various ribbons to see how many different effects can be achieved.

The exciting part of ribbon embroidery is the speed of the technique and to make it even more fun, play with fabric paint as a base and create highlights of ribbon embroidery. Enjoy the free style element of ribbon embroidery and create your own special magic.

Keep creating ....

Lesley Turpin-Delport

P.S. Use the small sketches in the corners for extra designs in silk ribbon embroidery.

CHAPTER ONE

WORKING WITH SILK RIBBON

Embroidery with silk ribbon is fun and quick to do. The stitches used are the same as those used in traditional embroidery floss, but the silk ribbon gives the stitches exciting dimensions.

Keep the ribbon flat as it is threaded in and out of the fabric, and control the tension on the ribbon and you will be thrilled with the result.

Needles
You can use a selection of crewel, chenille and tapestry needles but I prefer a chenille needle (24 or 26) which has an elongated eye and a sharp point. The ribbon threads easily into the eye of a chenille needle which perforates the fabric and allows the ribbon to pass easily through the background fabric.

Length of Ribbon
Cut the ribbon, at an angle, of approx. 30cm (12") in length. Too long a ribbon will fray and twist, which will not enhance your embroidery. To thread the needle; thread the ribbon through the eye of the needle, pull the ribbon through approx. 5cm (2") and pierce the ribbon 1cm ($\frac{1}{2}$") from the end. Pull the long end of the ribbon downwards until the ribbon locks into the eye of the needle. This prevents the needle from unthreading while you work.

How to begin and end
I like to work with a muslin foundation behind the background fabric. This is not always necessary but usually gives the work more body and also allows for a neat ending. Begin by leaving a small tail hanging at the back of your work. As you make your first stitch, pierce the tail with the needle to secure the ribbon. Some needle women find the tail securing difficult while doing tricky combinations. If this is the case make a small backstitch in the muslin foundation and through the tail of the ribbon.

Do not jump from one part of the design to another, as the colour might show through the background fabric. To prevent puckering, you should work with a small 10cm (4") embroidery ring.

To finish off your stitch
Take the ribbon through to the back and work a small backstitch into the muslin foundation and through the ribbon. Be careful not to snag the embroidered ribbon in that area. **OR** leave a tail which can be caught in when the next thread is started.

TIPS FOR SILK RIBBON EMBROIDERY

Do remember at all times that you are working with ribbon.

(1) Simple embroidery stitches work best with ribbon.

(2) Manipulate the ribbon correctly.

(3) The flat face of the ribbon should be laid down smoothly, without twists.

(4) Keep the ribbon thread short.

(5) Use your left thumb to hold the ribbon flat, and only release the thumb as you complete the stitch.

(6) You can hold the ribbon in place, when making certain stitches, with a pin or tapestry needle.

(7) Make sure that the ribbon is evenly spread once you have pulled it through the base fabric.

(8) To spread the ribbon, bring the needle through the fabric, hold the ribbon flat with the left thumb and slide the needle under the ribbon, towards the exit point. This should flatten the ribbon if you have used the correct needle to allow the ribbon to pass easily through the hole created by the needle. See sketch (a).

Butterflies Work in progress – this sample shows a mixture of silk ribbon and crewel embroidery, ideal for butterfly wings. Weaving, colonial knots, split stitch and inverted stab all work well together. *(Paulette Hodes)*

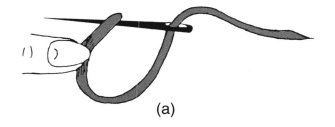

(a)

SIMPLE STITCH COMBINATIONS FOR SILK RIBBON EMBROIDERY

Running stitch

Whipped running stitch

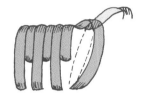

Long and short satin stitch

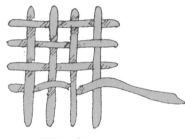

Weaving

Stem

Seed stitch

Couching

STAB STITCH

These are single spaced stitches worked either in a regular or irregular manner. Sometimes the stitches are of varying size. The stitches should be neither too long nor too loose. This stitch may also be worked on evenweave fabrics.

DETACHED CHAIN (LAZY DAISY)

Make a single chain stitch and anchor it with a small straight stitch. Five small detached chain stitches arranged like a flower make a daisy – hence the nick-name "lazy daisy"

IRIS STITCH

Make a single chain stitch and anchor it with a small straight stitch. Bring the ribbon through the fabric on the lower right of the chain. Using the back of the needle, slip the ribbon under the base of the chain loop. Anchor the ribbon on the lower left of the chain stitch, re-entering the background at this point. Make a yellow colonial knot or bullion in the centre of the chain.

SATIN STITCH

This stitch looks easy but it takes practise to make it perfect. The stitches should fit close together with very smooth or straight edges. The stitch may be straight or slanted. For large areas use a long and a short satin stitch for delicate shading. See page 9.

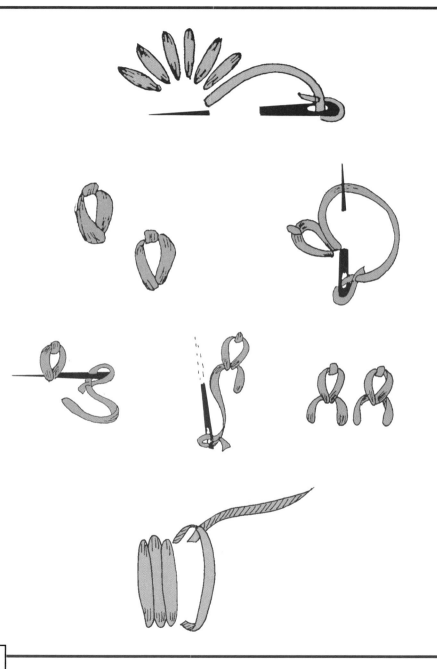

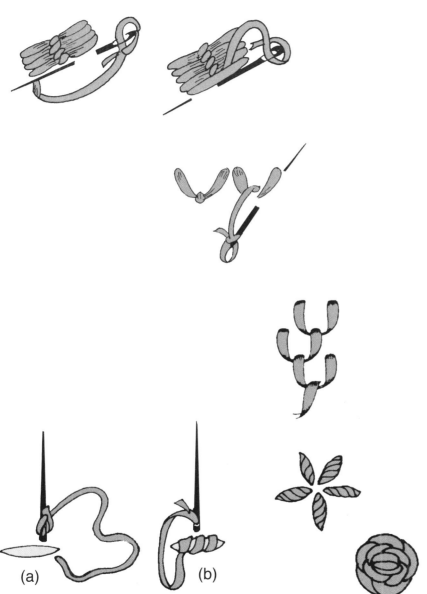

ROMANIAN STITCH
This is a satin stitch held down with a smaller, slanting stitch in the centre. The stitch can be worked very closely or further apart.

FLY STITCH
This can be very similar to Romanian except that the "V" shape is more marked. Make a satin stitch but come up in the centre of the stitch at a diagonal. Pull through and anchor the stitch with a small tying stitch.

FEATHER STITCH
Work a single feather stitch. The base of the first stitch forms the branch of the second stitch. Work a stitch to the left on the same level and then to the right. Continue working these two movements alternately.

MOCK BULLION (IDEAL FOR ROSES AND DAISIES)
Make a stab stitch as your foundation. (a) Use the back of the needle and wrap the ribbon around the stab stitch, three to four times, moving along the stitch. (b) Turn around at the top of the stitch and wrap the stab stitch three to four times again, moving down the stitch length.

(a)

(b)

COLONIAL KNOT

Pull the ribbon through the fabric. Place the needle under the ribbon, sliding the needle from left to right. (1)

Wrap the ribbon over the top of the needle from right to left creating a figure eight. (2)

Insert the needle into the fabric close to where it emerged; pull the working ribbon taut with your left hand so that a firm tight knot is formed. (3)

Pull the needle to the wrong side of the fabric forming a colonial knot. Come up at the next dot. (4)

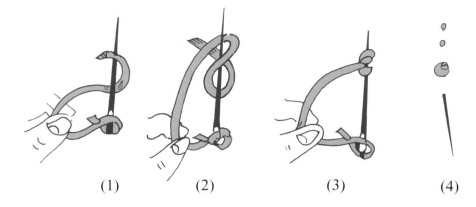

(1)　　　　(2)　　　　(3)　　　　(4)

SILK RIBBON FLOWER COMBINATIONS

COLONIAL KNOT AND STEM STITCH ROSE

Work 3 colonial knots for the centre, using the darkest shade of ribbon: Do not pull the ribbon too tightly, thus keeping a soft raised centre. Work stem stitch around the knotted centre, working in a clockwise direction, with the ribbon above the needle. Take a small pick-up stitch when making your stem stitch and slightly overlap the petal shapes as you proceed around the first circuit.

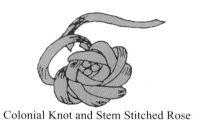

Colonial Knot and Stem Stitched Rose

Colonial Knot: Forget-Me-Not

LILY OF THE VALLEY

The flowers are a combination of lazy daisy and flystitch in silk ribbon with overcast stem and romanian leaves in embroidery floss.

CROSSED CHAIN ROSE
Bring the ribbon through the background fabric at point (a). Push the needle through the fabric at point (b) and exit at point (c), passing the ribbon beneath the needle tip creating a crossed chain. Pull though. Now slip the needle under the top right hand branch of the crossed chain. These two movements create the centre of the rose. Continue working around the rose centre, making crossed chains in an anti-clockwise direction. You can change colour to a paler shade as the rose grows in size.

TWIST AND SWIRL ROSE (KOEKSISTER)
Bring a short length of ribbon approx. 25cm (10") through the background fabric. Twist the needle between your thumb and middle finger causing the ribbon to twist. Once the ribbon is evenly twisted, insert the tip of the needle into the fabric, allowing the ribbon to swirl back on itself, like a plait (or koeksister). Gently pull the concertina-shaped ribbon through the fabric, stopping when you have a perfect rose shape. Secure the delicate rose with matching thread to stabilise the shape. Add green fly stitch in two strands of embroidery floss, to the outer edge of the rose, creating a suggestion of thorns.

ROSEBUDS
The rosebud is a combination of a colonial knot surrounded by a lazy daisy.

Rosebuds

SNOWDROPS
This flower is a combination of three lazy daisies in silk ribbon with a bullion calyx and extended french knot stamens in embroidery floss.

Snowdrops

LOOPED 3D PETAL DAISIES

Make the looped daisies last as they are rather fragile. Cut a 20cm (8") length of ribbon for each daisy. Do not remove the pins until the base of each petal is secured with a colonial knot (or french knot) in two strands of yellow embroidery floss. The centre can be embellished with extra french knots or stamens in extended french knots. (See crewel stitch glossary on pages 22-24).

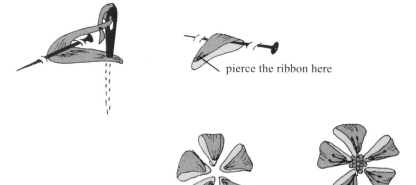

pierce the ribbon here

anchored colonial knot

NAMAQUALAND DAISIES

These daisies are made using an *inverted stab stitch*. Bring the needle through the background fabric and at the tip of the petal pierce the ribbon and the fabric in the same movement. Pull the ribbon gently through forming a "nipped" tip. Stabilise each petal with a stab stitch in two strands of embroidery floss. Fill the centre with small french knots.

For a daisy bud, make a single inverted stab stitch in silk, secured with a floss stab stitch and an extended fly stitch calyx.

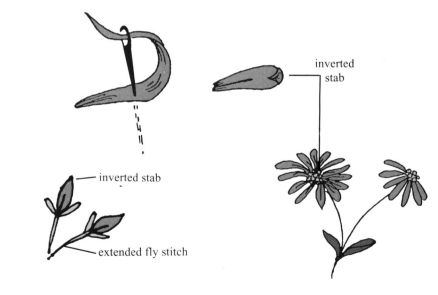

inverted stab

inverted stab

extended fly stitch

EXCITING CREWEL AND SILK RIBBON COMBINATIONS

Buttonhole stitch

Buttonhole stitch wheel

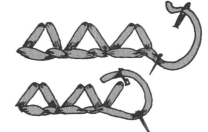

Closed buttonhole

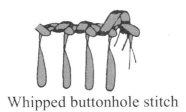

Whipped buttonhole stitch

Buttonhole, lazy daisy and french knots

Closed buttonhole, french knot and stab

Feather stitch

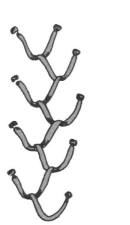

Feather stitch and beads

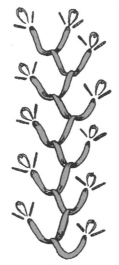

Feather stitch, lazy daisy
and stab stitch

Feather stitch, lazy daisy and
french knot

EXCITING CREWEL AND SILK RIBBON COMBINATIONS

Cross stitch

Fishbone

Whipped spiders web

Lazy daisy

Lazy daisy, stab stitch and french knot

Chain stitch

Lazy daisy, stab stitch and french knot

Chevron

Chevron, french knot and lazy daisy

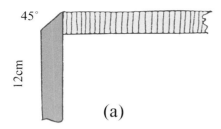

CHAPTER TWO

45°

12cm

(a)

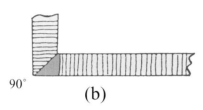

90°

(b)

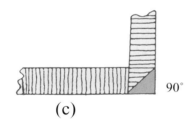

90°

(c)

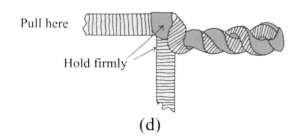

Pull here

Hold firmly

(d)

WORKING WITH SATIN RIBBON

HOW TO MAKE SATIN RIBBON ROSES

Thread a needle with matching sewing machine thread before you begin.

The FULL BLOWN or *JACK-IN-THE-BOX* rose is made by folding the ribbon in half at 45 degrees, approximately 12cm (4½") along the ribbon length. Do not cut the ribbon yet. (a)

Then fold the top piece backwards to form a square. (b)

Now fold the right hand length, backwards to continue the square shape. (c)

Continue folding backwards at 90 degrees using up the full length. Hold the last ribbon fold firmly on itself and pull the other length to form the rose shape. *Do not pull too hard, otherwise you will lose the rose shape.* Stitch the base firmly through the centre a couple of times, so that the rose feels secure. Do not cut the rose off the ribbon length, until you have made a couple of roses, to prevent ribbon waste. (d)

THE CABBAGE ROSE
(Or Tab Method)

Cut a short length of ribbon approx 6cm (2¼"). This is the tab. Fold the tab over the end of the ribbon length, forming a square with the ribbon. (a)

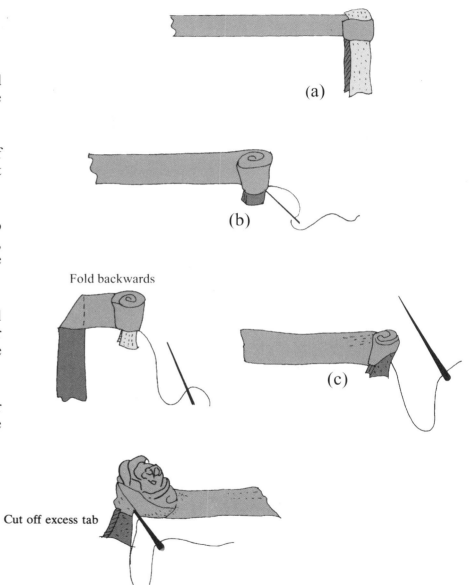

(a)

Form the bud centre of the rose by rolling the ribbon tightly on itself a few times, making a tight tube. Make a couple of small stitches at the base to hold it firm. (b)

(b)

To form the petals, fold the ribbon backwards so that it is parallel to the tube, forming a 45 degree angle. Roll the tube across the fold, loosely at the top and tightly at the base. Stitch in place with a couple of stitches. (c)

Fold backwards

Continue to fold, roll and stitch, shaping the roses as you work, until it is the desired size. Finish by turning the raw end under the rose or sear the ribbon by quickly passing it under the base of a candle flame.

(c)

Once you have made a selection of roses, position them onto your background fabric and stitch them in place with tiny, invisible stitches.

Cut off excess tab

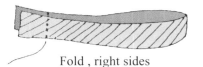

Fold , right sides
facing inwards

Fold around
inverted, gathered centre

TINY RIBBON ROSEBUD

Ribbon approx 8 - 10mm wide ($\frac{3}{8}$" - $\frac{1}{2}$"). Cut a length of ribbon approx 12cm ($4\frac{1}{2}$") long. Fold the ribbon in half, lengthwise, right sides together. Run a gathering thread along the narrow side, about 3mm ($\frac{1}{8}$") from the raw ends. Turn the loop to the right side and start to roll the rosebud centre in a firm tube by folding the double ribbon over to the right and wrapping tightly around the solid centre. Stitch firmly and once you have a nice centre, make a 45 degree backward fold and roll. Stitch again and complete the bud by folding, rolling and stitching.

LARGE FLAMBOYANT ROSES

To create these extravagant roses use wide ribbon approx 2 - 3cm (1") in three different shades; darker ribbons for the centre of the flower and paler ribbons for the outer petals. The centre of the rose is made using the tab method (see page 18). The rest of the petals are made separately using a *trapezoid* shape.

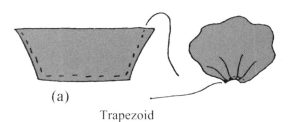

(a)

Trapezoid

Cut *three lengths* of medium coloured ribbon, 8cm (3") on the long side and *five lengths* of the paler ribbon approx 8cm (3") on the long side. Sear the diagonal sides under a flame to prevent unravelling. Gather each piece of ribbon with small running stitches. (see illustration (a)) Stitch the first three petals around the centre of the rose, slightly overlapping each petal (b). Complete the rose by stitching the five pale petals around the centre shape, again slightly overlapping each petal   (c). Stitch the completed rose onto the background fabric, checking that all the stitches are hidden. The rose must be good looking from all angles.

Once you have mastered this rose, enjoy it's potential and play with different ribbons and numbers of petals.

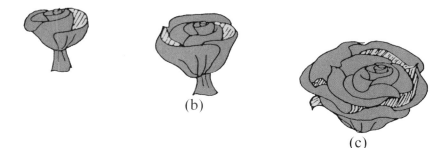

(b)

(c)

SATIN RIBBON LEAVES

Using ribbons approx 1.5cm ($^5/_8$") wide, cut a rectangle of ribbon approx 8cm ($3^1/_4$") in length. Sear the raw ends by passing the ribbon through the base of a flame. Fold the top corners to the centre to form a mitred triangle. See sketch (a). Run a gathering thread along the seared edges. Pull the gathers up firmly to form the leaf shape (b). Tuck this edge under the rose and stitch it firmly to the background. For a stronger leaf, use a double thread brought through the tip of the leaf and secure it into the background (c).

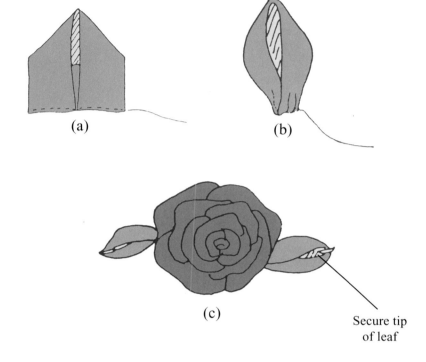

(a)

(b)

(c)

Secure tip of leaf

LARGE ROSEBUD WITH CALYX

Use the tab method (see page 18) to create the rosebud, ribbon approx 2cm ($^3/_4$") wide. Make the leaf shape as described above (a), and tuck the tab method rosebud into the calyx shape. Manipulate the petals and the calyx into an attractive shape as you attach it to the background.

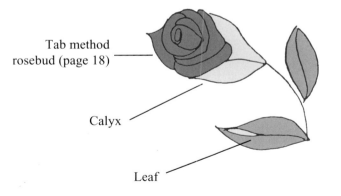

Tab method rosebud (page 18)

Calyx

Leaf

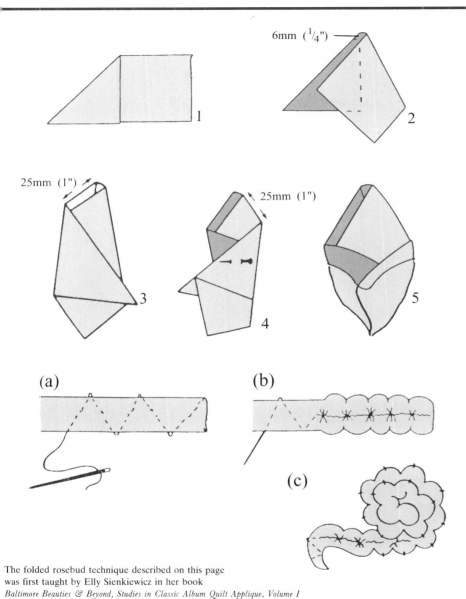

FOLDED ROSEBUDS

Make folded rosebuds from a rectangle of ribbon approx 2cm x 7.5cm ($^3/_4$" x 3").

1.   Fold the left side down at right angles to the centre.

2.   Fold the right side down so that it runs parallel to the diagonal left side, leaving a small space 6mm ($^1/_4$").

3.   Fold the left side from the left to the right at an angle, about 25mm (1") from the point.

4.   Fold the right hand side, from right to left at an angle, about 2mm (1") from the point and secure the cross-over with a pin or a stitch. Trim the base of the folded rose to fit neatly into the calyx.

5.   Pin the folded edges in place and applique the calyx to the rosebud. Hem the outer edge of the rose to the background but leave the inner fold of the bud free.

RUCHED RIBBON

Ruched ribbon can be used to make zinnias, full-blown roses or chrysanthemums. Work running stitches in a zigzag along the length of the ribbon strip. (a) Pull up to gather until you have a well ruched strip. (b) Begin the appliqueing of the ribbon in the centre and work outwards, underlapping the shapes as you proceed. Secure the ribbon with one stitch on each scallop. (c)

The folded rosebud technique described on this page was first taught by Elly Sienkiewicz in her book
Baltimore Beauties & Beyond, Studies in Classic Album Quilt Applique, Volume I
(1989 C&T Publishing, Martinez, CA 94553, USA)
The method for ruching is also illustrated in the same book.
Both methods are shared here with Elly's permission.

CREWEL STITCH GLOSSARY
Ideal with satin and silk ribbon

Chain Stitch

Stem Stitch

Back Stitch

Buttonhole Stitch

Detached Chain Stitch
(Lazy Daizy)

Satin Stitch

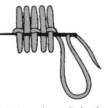

Weaving Stitch

Long and Short Satin Stitch

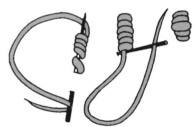

Bullion Knot

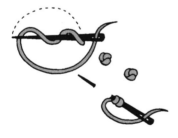

French Knot

Extended French Knot

Feather Stitch

Couching

Bullion Rose

Grub Rose

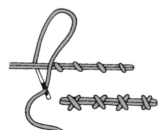

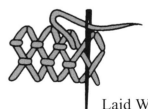

Laid Work

CREWEL STITCH GLOSSARY
Ideal with satin and silk ribbon

Whipped Spider's Web

Woven Spider's Web
Even Spokes

Woven Spider's Web
Uneven Spokes

Split Stitch (2 Strands)

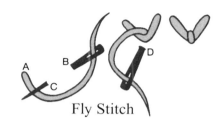

Fly Stitch

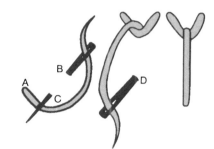

Extended Fly Stitch

Portuguese Border
Stitch

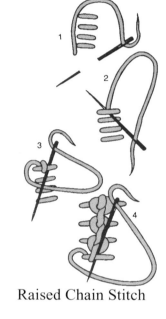

Raised Chain Stitch

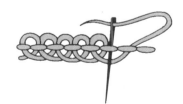

Romanian Stitch

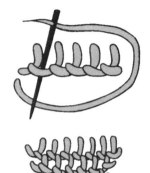

Semi-detached
Buttonhole

Whipped Chain

Pekinese Stitch

CREWEL STITCH GLOSSARY
Ideal with satin and silk ribbon

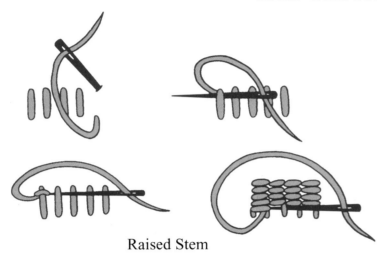

Raised Stem

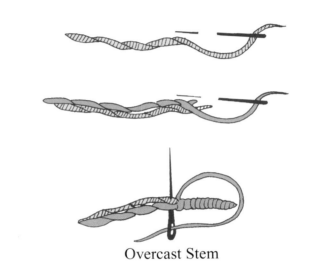

Overcast Stem

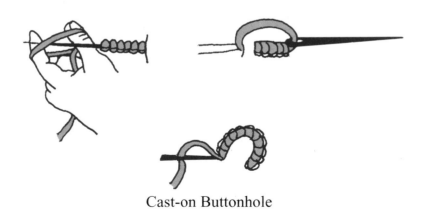

Cast-on Buttonhole

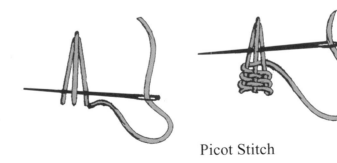

Picot Stitch

PROJECTS

SATIN RIBBON POSY

3D satin roses and candlewick lace flowers combine to create a charming posy.

MATERIALS

Background fabric
Muslin
Satin ribbon approx. 8 or 10mm ($^3/_8$")
Matching embroidery thread and green embroidery thread for leaves and stems.
White candlewick thread No 8
Crewel needle for embroidery
Chenille needle for candlewicking

INSTRUCTIONS

Refer to the glossary on pages 22 - 24 and the sketch opposite.

All the embroidery is in two strands of embroidery floss. Lightly sketch the design onto the background fabric. Tack the muslin behind this background fabric. Begin by embroidering the bow, in the colour matching your rosebuds in *raised stem*. Then begin the victorian lace flower using the *colonial knot* in white No 8 thread with the chenille needle (or use the *french knot* and *extended french knots*). The lace flower stalks are in *fine backstitch* ending with fronds of *stab stitch*. Scattered in between the satin ribbon roses are *bullion rosebuds*. Make one, *six twist bullion* in the centre, in the rose colour, with an *eight twist bullion* on each side of it and finish off with a *ten twist bullion* in green on either side. The stems of the Victorian lace flower are in green *backstitch* and the stems of the satin ribbon roses are in *overcast stem*. Make a selection of satin ribbon roses and attach each rose to the background with small invisible stitches.

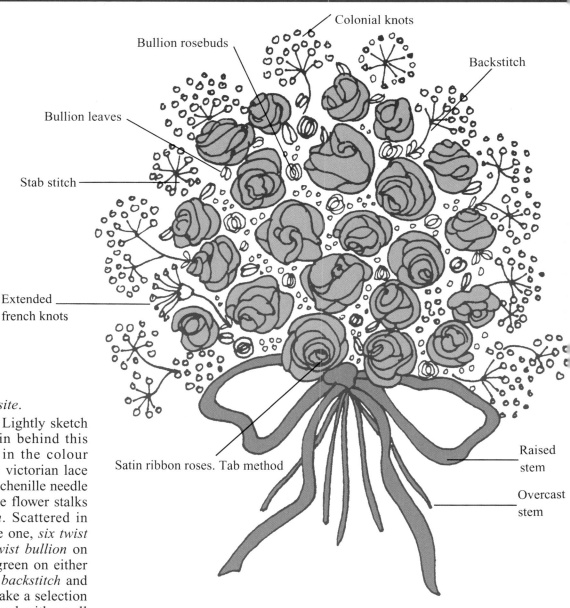

Colonial knots

Bullion rosebuds

Backstitch

Bullion leaves

Stab stitch

Extended french knots

Satin ribbon roses. Tab method

Raised stem

Overcast stem

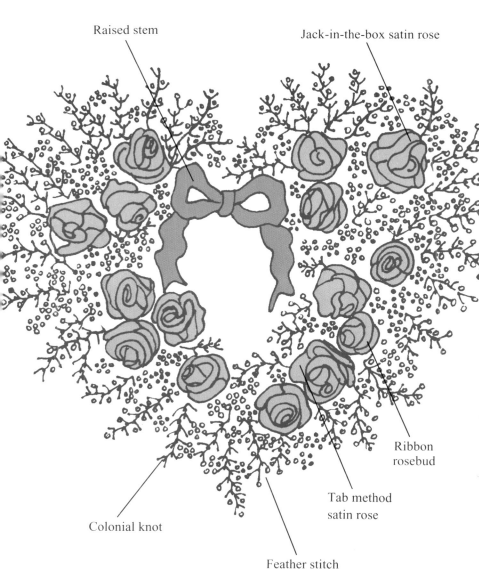

Raised stem

Jack-in-the-box satin rose

Ribbon rosebud

Tab method satin rose

Colonial knot

Feather stitch

SATIN RIBBON HEART

Peach blossoms and antique satin ribbon roses combine to make a perfect heart. Romantic and frivolous this design make a delightful cushion or framed picture.

MATERIALS
Background fabric
Muslin
Satin ribbon approx. 8 or 10mm ($^3/_8$")
Matching embroidery thread and green embroidery thread for leaves and stems.
White candlewick thread No 8
Crewel needle for embroidery
Chenille needle for candlewicking

INSTRUCTIONS
Refer to the glossary on pages 22 - 24 and the sketch opposite.

All the embroidery is in two strands of embroidery thread. Lightly sketch the design onto the background fabric. Tack the muslin behind the marked background fabric. Begin by embroidering the bow, in *raised stem*. Move onto the foliage, in green, using *feather stitch*. Use white candlewick thread and the chenille needle to make white buds, with *colonial knots*. Start at the tip of the branch and work inwards. Use the photograph (page 28) as your guide. For the blossoms make one *colonial knot* in the centre and work around it with 5 *colonial knots*. Scatter this combination around the basic heart shape. Play with the 3D satin ribbon rose techniques and make up your own interesting combinations. Arrange them onto the background fabric and attach each rose securely with small invisible stitches.

Victorian Rose Collection

Left: **Bottle-green and cream victorian rose collection.** Hearts, posies and bouquets are the essence of romance, softened with gypsophila, rosebuds and blossoms.

Below: **Satin Ribbon Heart.** Blossoms in colonial knots and a raised stem bow compliment the delicate satin ribbon roses on a rich, bottle-green background. Frame the heart design as a picture with a pair of mix-and-match, beautifully ruched and piped cushions. *(Anne Neill)*

Top right: **Satin Ribbon Posy.** Old rose pink, double sided ribbon from Czechoslovakia fold softly to form these rich rosebuds. Try a number of different satin ribbon rose methods to create a variety of roses. *(Lesley Turpin-Delport)*

Bottom right: **Satin Ribbon Posy on bottle-green.** A grained linen background provides a strong contrast for the ecru roses and off-white gypsophila. *(Anne Neill)*

Far right: **Satin Ribbon Posy.** An interesting variation on a theme. Lilacs and strong pinks are frivolous and festive in comparison with the 'old worlde' and sophisticated loo of the other colour combinations. *(Susan Sittig)*

**3 Satin Ribbon
Posies**

SHADES OF SUMMER

POSY DESIGN

Silk ribbon, and a dash of embroidery, combine to create a profusion of summer flowers. Have fun and make up your posy into a frilled cushion, or frame it for your favourite summer time patio.

MATERIALS

Background fabric
Muslin
Two needles: one crewel for traditional embroidery, one chenille for silk embroidery.
No 8 white candlewick thread
A selection of silk ribbon in shades of summer.
A selection of embroidery thread (light and dark green and yellow.)

INSTRUCTIONS

Refer to the glossary on pages 22 - 24 and the sketch opposite.

Lightly pencil the design onto the white cotton background. Tack the muslin behind the background fabric. Part of the design is in traditional embroidery. The stems of the posy are in two strands of green embroidery floss in *overcast stem*. The gypsophila is in No 8 white candlewicking thread using *colonial knots*. The stalks of the gypsophila are in two strands of dark green in *stab stitch*. The rest of the design is in silk ribbon embroidery (see Chapter 1). Make the looped daisies last as they are rather fragile. Secure these 3D petals in two strands of yellow embroidery floss with *colonial knots* in the centre and *extended french knot* stamens. Once all the embroidery is complete, make a bow from the left over silk ribbon. Stitch the bow securely to the posy at the top of the stalks.

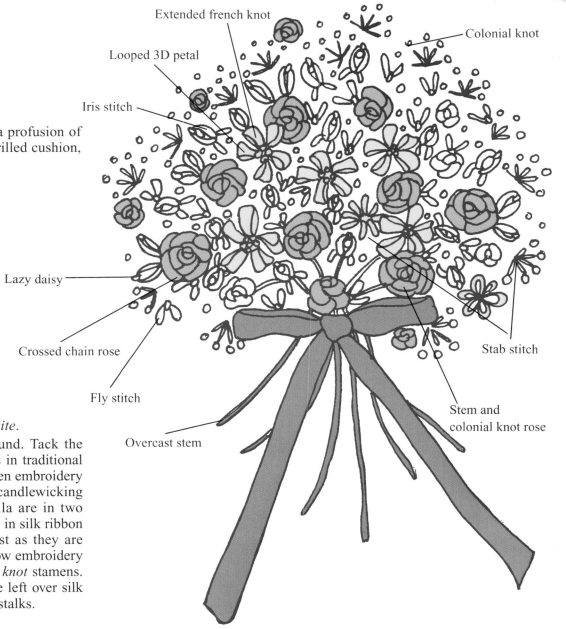

Extended french knot

Colonial knot

Looped 3D petal

Iris stitch

Lazy daisy

Crossed chain rose

Fly stitch

Stab stitch

Stem and colonial knot rose

Overcast stem

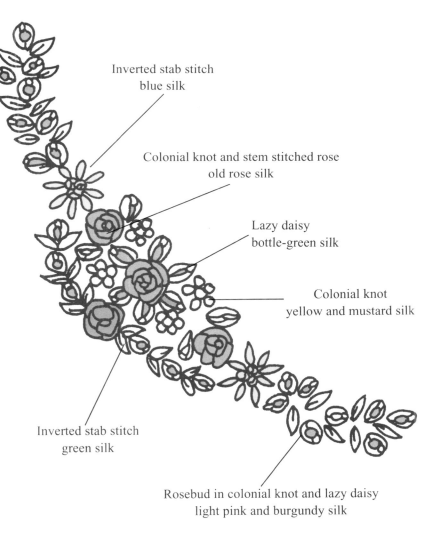

Inverted stab stitch
blue silk

Colonial knot and stem stitched rose
old rose silk

Lazy daisy
bottle-green silk

Colonial knot
yellow and mustard silk

Inverted stab stitch
green silk

Rosebud in colonial knot and lazy daisy
light pink and burgundy silk

DINNER NAPKIN

Make a set of silk embroidered napkins to enhance a special dinner party table. A single napkin looks delightful as a traycloth or teapot holder.

MATERIALS

Purchase a white napkin with lace trim or make a napkin 40 x 40cm (16" x 16") and edge it with crisp white lace. A selection of silk ribbon for roses and daisies. Chenille needle No 22/24

INSTRUCTIONS

Refer to the glossary on pages 22 - 24 and the sketch opposite.

Sketch the design onto the corner of your napkin with a pencil. The roses are *colonial knot* and *stem stitch* combinations, with buds of *colonial knots* surrounded by *lazy daisy*. The tiny daisies are *colonial knots*; one mustard knot in the centre of five pale yellow knots. The large daisies are *inverted stab stitch* in blue silk with three mustard *colonial knots* in the centre. The bottle-green leaves are *lazy daisy* while the light green leaves are *inverted stab stitch*.

Shades of Summer

Shades of Summer. Pure silk and white cotton suggests a summerhouse luncheon or a picnic in the romantic style of DH Lawrence. *(Rachelle Druian, Nikki Delport, Sandra Caister and Anne Neill)*.

Posy detail. What wonderful texture and dimension can be achieved with silk embroidered flowers. *(Blanche Sessel)*.

Tea set. Dress up a plain napkin with a quick and easy design to compliment a charming porcelain tea set. *(Nikki Delport)*

Inset is the napkin detail. Simple silk embroidery stitches are clearly visible in this detail of the napkin.

·sy. Eau de nil, cinnamon and 'funky' tones gleam with a ~~ken~~ sheen in the late afternoon sunlight.

HEXAGON TRINKET BOX

This quilted and embroidered box is made up from small pieces of prequilted fabric with a touch of hand embroidery on the lid. It is ideal for antique jewellery or precious trinkets.

MATERIALS
Cardboard templates
0.25 metre (10") of pre-quilted fabric
0.25 metre (10") of toning cotton fabric for the lining
0.25 metre (10") of polyester wadding for padding
Matching sewing thread
Lipstick type glue
A selection of silk ribbon

BASIC CONSTRUCTION

The box is made up of six panels, and a hexagon for the base of the box; six narrow panels and a larger hexagon for the lid.

THE BASE

Place the *six large cardboard templates* on the *lining fabric* and draw around the shapes with a soft pencil. Cut out the fabric shapes, leaving 1cm ($^3/_8$") seam allowance around each shape. Cut out the *lining* and quilted fabric for the base *hexagon template* with the same 1cm ($^3/_8$") allowance. Mark the polyester wadding and cut it out; the same size as the six panels and hexagon template. Spread the lipstick glue onto the cardboard and stick a piece of the polyester wadding onto each shape.

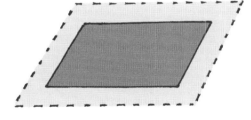

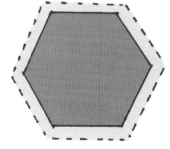

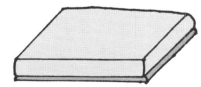

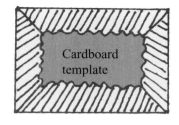

Cardboard template

Fabric folded over to wrong side

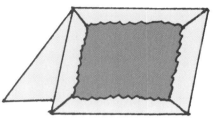

Whip fabric-covered templates together

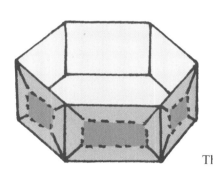

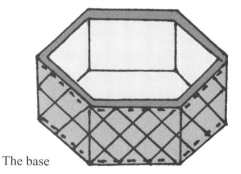

The base

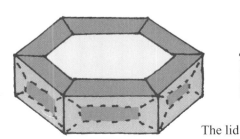

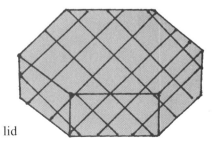

The lid

Cover each panel with the lining fabric by folding the 1cm ($^3/_8$") seam allowance over to the wrong side. Lightly glue with the lipstick glue.

Sew the outside panels together, hemming through the material only.

Cover the hexagon base panel and oversew it to the sides.

Cut a length of prequilted fabric 10 x 55 cm ($3^3/_4$" x $21^3/_4$") for the outside of the base. With right sides together, seam the two short ends together checking that the material can slip over the basic hexagon construction and fit snugly together. Slip the quilted fabric over the base and see that 1cm ($^3/_8$") seam allowance protrudes on the upper and lower edge. Fold the 1cm ($^3/_8$") seam allowance on the lower edge over to the under side of the hexagon and glue the allowance down with the lipstick glue.

Trim away a little at the corners, if necessary. Fold the 1cm ($^3/_8$") seam allowance under the upper edge, pin and stab stitch the lining and quilted edges together. Spread a little glue on the hexagon base panel and stick the pre-quilted hexagon fabric in place. Fold under the 1cm ($^3/_8$") seam allowance, pin and stab stitch the folded edges together, pinching the fabric as you proceed.

THE LID

Cut out the fabric and cover the six narrow templates and the lid hexagon with the wadding and lining fabric only, as described in the base section. Whip the side panels and hexagon together to form the lid shape. (The procedure is the same as in the base instructions) Cut out the prequilted hexagon for the outside of the lid with a 1cm ($^3/_8$") seam allowance.

Cut a strip of prequilted fabric 6 x 61cm ($2^3/_8$" x 24") for the outside of the side panels. With right sides together, seam the two short ends together, checking that the material can slip over the basic hexagon shape. The seam allowance must protrude on both sides. Fold the 1cm ($^3/_8$") seam allowance over at the lip edge, pin and stab stitch the lining and prequilted fabric together.

Now fold the left over seam allowance over onto the hexagon and glue the fabric onto the cardboard. Trim a little fabric away at each corner point until the fabric fits snugly onto the cardboard.

Embroider the outside hexagon fabric with the silk ribbon design of roses and daisies (see Chapter I Silk Embroidery) or the design below

A piece of wadding can be placed between the cardboard of the lid and the embroidered hexagon. Turn under the seam allowance, pin the hexagon and side edges together and stab stitch through all the layers. Keep your stitches tiny and neat as this forms the outer edge of the lid of the box.

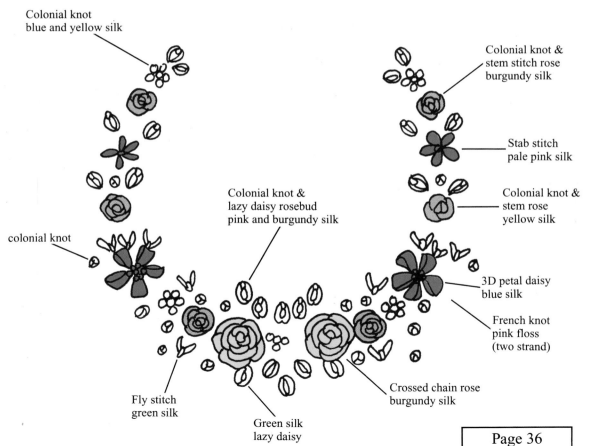

Colonial knot
blue and yellow silk

colonial knot

Colonial knot &
lazy daisy rosebud
pink and burgundy silk

Fly stitch
green silk

Green silk
lazy daisy

Crossed chain rose
burgundy silk

French knot
pink floss
(two strand)

3D petal daisy
blue silk

Colonial knot &
stem rose
yellow silk

Stab stitch
pale pink silk

Colonial knot &
stem stitch rose
burgundy silk

Trinket Box made from cardboard, quilted cotton and a little silk embroidery *(Rachelle Druian)*

Floral Wreath This is another design which could be used for the lid of a trinket box *(Susan Sittig)*

A TRINKET BOX TEMPLATE

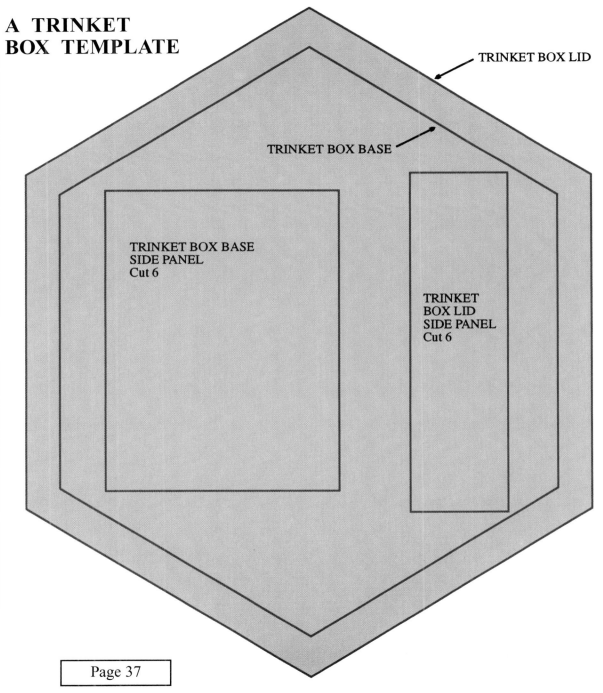

TRINKET BOX LID

TRINKET BOX BASE

TRINKET BOX BASE
SIDE PANEL
Cut 6

TRINKET
BOX LID
SIDE PANEL
Cut 6

lk Heart This design is another idea for the lid of a trinket box. lovely gift for a precious friend. *(Sue Druckman)*

lk Heart detail How splendid a simple heart appears in pure lk flowers and traditional embroidery,

WICKER BASKET SERIES

ROSES AND DAISIES

This is a delightful cameo combining traditional embroidery and the third dimension of silk and satin ribbon.

INSTRUCTIONS

Refer to the glossary on pages 22 - 24 and the sketch opposite.

Lightly pencil the design onto your background fabric. Tack the muslin behind the fabric for a strong foundation. Use the sketch and the photographs as your guide and the cameo will grow as you create the different flowers. Part of the design is in traditional embroidery: The stems are in two strands of green floss in *whipped backstitch*. The leaves are *bullion knots* (two strands of dark green floss) and *lazy daisy* (two strands of light green floss) and *romanian* (two strands of light green)

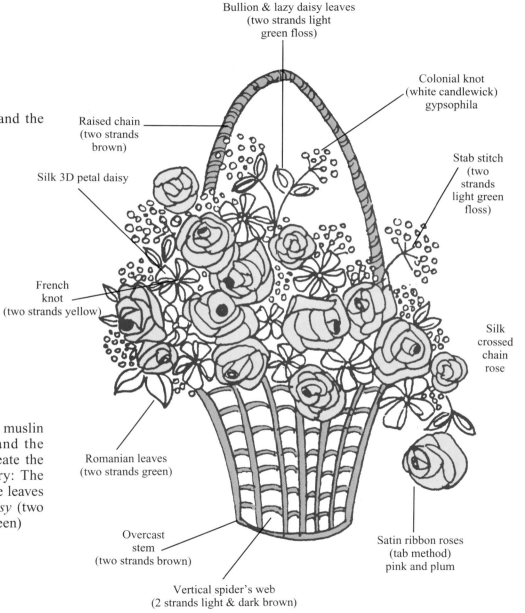

Bullion & lazy daisy leaves
(two strands light
green floss)

Colonial knot
(white candlewick)
gypsophila

Raised chain
(two strands
brown)

Stab stitch
(two
strands
light green
floss)

Silk 3D petal daisy

French
knot
(two strands yellow)

Silk
crossed
chain
rose

Romanian leaves
(two strands green)

Overcast
stem
(two strands brown)

Satin ribbon roses
(tab method)
pink and plum

Vertical spider's web
(2 strands light & dark brown)

The gypsophila is in No 8 white candlewicking thread using *colonial knots*. The stalks of the gypsophila are in two strands of green embroidery floss in *stab stitch*.

The wicker basket is made up of a combination of *vertical spider's web* (two strands of light brown floss in the centre, changing to dark at the outer edges) and *overcast stem*. (Two strands of dark brown floss).

The handle of the wicker basket is in *raised chain* (two strands of dark brown floss).

Now study the methods for making satin ribbon roses. (page 17)
Once you have made a selection of roses, position them onto your background fabric and stitch them in place. The rest of the design is in silk ribbon embroidery. The daisies are 3D looped petals in white silk ribbon with yellow *french knot* centres.

Rose Filigree, ideal for framing, a beautiful cushion or monograms – adding a name in the centre for that personal touch.
All the stitches in this design are the same as those used in "Roses and Daisies"
(Susan Sittig)

Wicker Basket Series

Left:
Di's Basket is essentially pure silk ribbon embroidery which creates a bolder impression. The colours are stronger because of the primary choice.
(Di Thompson)

Left:
'Memories are made of this' – A mother recreates an image of her delightful daughter by transferring a photograph onto fabric and then embellishing it with silk flowers on her hat and wicker basket.
(Sue Ackerman)

Right:
Roses and Daisies. Satin and silk embroidery gives tremendous depth to this basket of roses and daisies.
(Susan Sittig)

ow right:

e's Basket is mainly one strand floss
broidery with highlights of silk ribbon flowers
usan Druckman) and below the detail.

Left:
Anne's Basket is made up of two strand floss
and flower thread embroidery with a few
accents of silk flowers. *(Anne Neill)*

Above:
Detail of the flower arrangement.

Right:
Renske's Hanging Basket. Flower thread
and silk combine to form a basket seen from a
different angle. *(Renske Biddulph)*

Sue's Basket

A selection of baskets for the reader to enjoy.

Refer to the Stitch Glossary on pages 22, 23 and 24 as well as the photographs on pages 40 and 41, and make up your own floral combinations

Anne's Basket

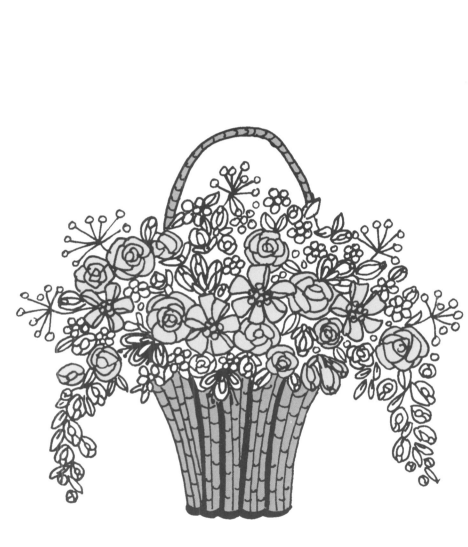

Di's Basket

Renske's Hanging Basket

Lovers Knot

Valentine Heart detail. Try a bottle-green background for something reall different. *(Susan Sittig)*

Valentine Heart detail. Rose pink provides a Victorian feel for the Valentine design. *(Susan Sittig)*

Valentine Heart. Here we have a wonderful mixture of satin, silk, candlewicking and traditional embroidery. The colours work well with any decor as peaches and cream have been combined with white and oyster. *(Susan Sittig)*.

Valentine Heart on Ecru. The satin and silk methods described in chapters I and II are clearly visible in this detail. *(Rachelle Druian)*

Valentine Heart in embroidery ring. Notice how the ring holds the fabric taut while you work. *(Rachelle Druian)*

Valentine Heart. Make up the heart into a frilled cushion using wide anglaise lace. *(Rachelle Druian)*

Page 45

LOVER'S KNOT

VALENTINE HEART

Satin and silk ribbon with embroidery creates a Lover's Knot of romantic flowers. Have fun and frame the antique heart in an exotic frame or make it up into a glorious cushion.

MATERIALS

Cotton background fabric 40 x 40cm (16 x 16")
Muslin 40 x 40cm (16 x 16")
Two needles: one crewel for traditional embroidery,
one chenille for silk embroidery
No 8 white candlewicking thread
A selection of silk ribbon: blue, oyster, green and white
A selection of embroidery thread: light green and yellow floss
A selection of satin ribbon: apricot and old rose 8/10mm
wide ($1/4$-$3/8$")

INSTRUCTIONS

On the bottle-green background fabric, transfer the design by using pale dressmaker's carbon.
OR
Cut out the heart shape, pin it onto the background fabric and tailor's tack the position of the flowers in different coloured threads. Use the sketch and the photographs as your guide and the flowered heart will grow as you create the different flowers.
OR
On a *pastel* background, lightly sketch the design onto the fabric with an HB pencil.

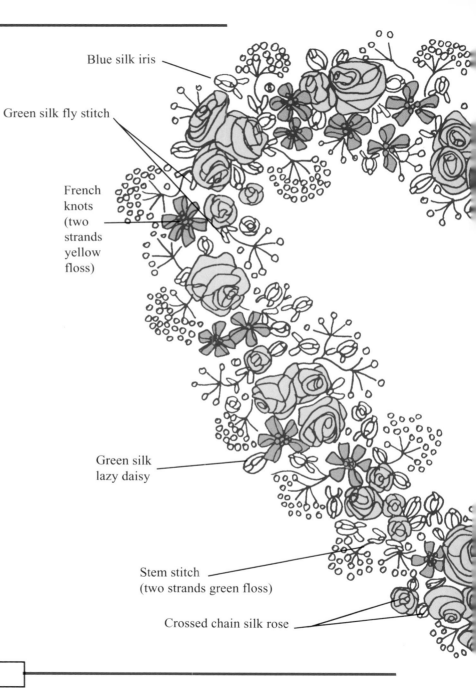

Blue silk iris

Green silk fly stitch

French knots (two strands yellow floss)

Green silk lazy daisy

Stem stitch (two strands green floss)

Crossed chain silk rose

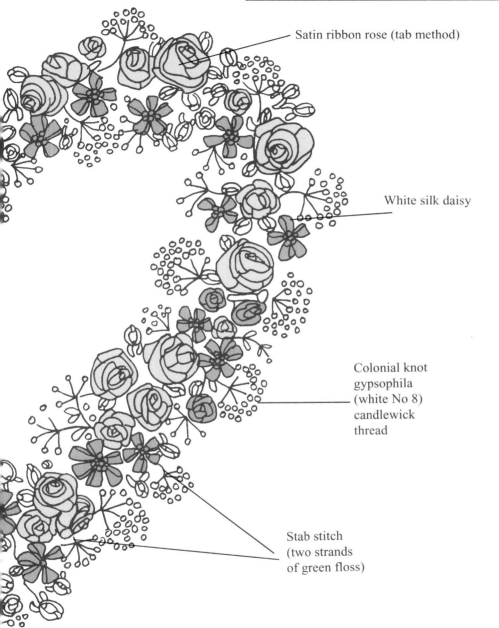

Satin ribbon rose (tab method)

White silk daisy

Colonial knot
gypsophila
(white No 8)
candlewick
thread

Stab stitch
(two strands
of green floss)

Part of the design is in *traditional embroidery*: (See stitch glossary)
The stems are in two strands of green embroidery floss in *stem stitch*.

The gypsophila is in No 8 white candlewicking thread using *colonial knots*.
The stalks of the gypsophila are in two strands of green floss in *stab stitch*.

Now study the methods for making *SATIN RIBBON ROSES* and use the *tab method* described on page 18 in rose pink and apricot satin ribbon.
Once you have made a selection of roses, position them onto your background fabric, according to the illustration and stitch them in place.

The rest of the design is in silk ribbon embroidery. Study the notes on silk ribbon stitches in Chapter 1 and begin an exciting embroidery experience.
The irises are in blue silk ribbon using *iris stitch*. Sometimes I insert a yellow *french knot* in the centre of the bloom. The roses are in oyster silk ribbon using the *crossed chain rose* or a *colonial knot* and *stem stitch* rose (See chapter I - Silk Ribbon Flower Combinations)

The 3D looped daisies are in white silk with yellow *french knot* centres.
The leaves are in green silk using *fly stitch* and *lazy daisy*

Midsummer-night's Dream

Left:

Wedding Dress. An unusual, pure silk wedding dress decorated with satin and silk in buttercup yellow, cornflower blue and shades of red. *(Beryl Soller)*

Inset: The detail clearly shows Namaqualand daisies, snowdrops and forget-me-nots in silk ribbon snuggled into a cluster of multi-coloured satin ribbon roses.

Below:

Rust antique handkerchief detail. Feather stitch and colonial knots soften the 3D petal daisies and satin roses. The rust handkerchief fabric is fine georgette. *(Susan Sittig)*

Right:

Basket and Bouquet. This still life was sketched onto the fabric with an indelible pen. Soft touches of colour in fabric paint provide a backdrop for the floral details in satin and silk. *(Sharlene Chimes)*

Inset bottom right: **Victorian Sampler rose pink background.** The Victorian sampler is a variation of the wedding dress theme. A gentle interpretation in pastel shades. *(Susan Sittig)*

Inset top: **Victorian Sampler detail.** A close up shows the simple construction of the different flowers. *(Susan Sittig)*

MIDSUMMER-NIGHT'S DREAM

WEDDING DRESS DESIGN

Create midsummer magic in an ochre silk wedding dress embellished with a cascade of satin and silk blooms.

MATERIALS

A selection of *satin* ribbon (10mm wide) ($^3/_8$")
Ecru, apricot, old rose, burgundy and cherry red.
A selection of *silk* ribbon. Ecru, apricot, blue, cherry red and shades of green and mustard.
Embroidery floss. Yellow, ecru, cherry red and green.
Two needles, chenille and crewel.
Chamois leather (for headband of veil)

INSTRUCTIONS

Sketch the design onto the bodice of the wedding dress. Reverse left and right. Study the labelled sketch and the photograph. Begin with the crewel embroidery, then the silk, and complete the cascade with a mixture of satin ribbon roses using the *tab method*.

HEADBAND

Purchase a headband and cover it with ochre chamoise leather. Decorate with chamoise roses by rolling and folding the chamoise at 45 degrees. Glue a selection of multi-coloured roses onto the headband.

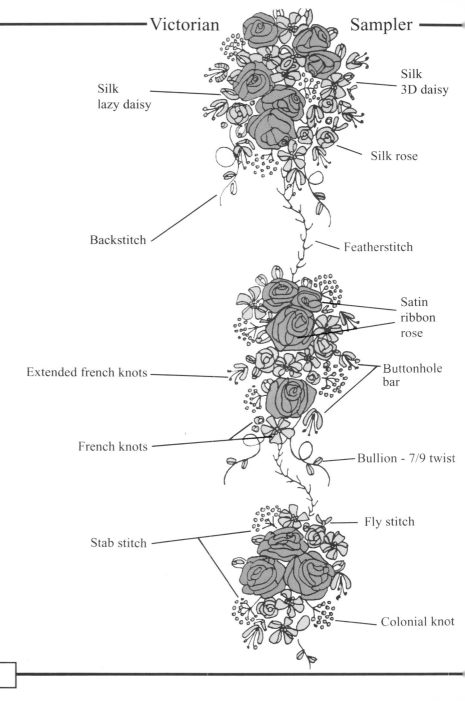

Silk lazy daisy

Silk 3D daisy

Silk rose

Backstitch

Featherstitch

Satin ribbon rose

Extended french knots

Buttonhole bar

French knots

Bullion - 7/9 twist

Stab stitch

Fly stitch

Colonial knot

WEDDING DRESS DESIGN - FORGET-ME-NOT

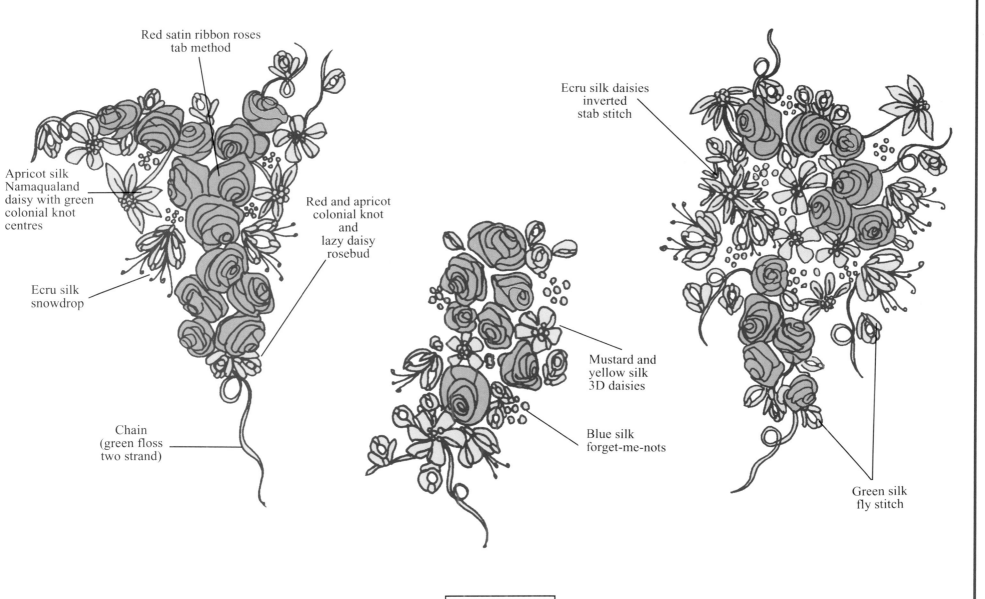

Red satin ribbon roses
tab method

Ecru silk daisies
inverted
stab stitch

Apricot silk
Namaqualand
daisy with green
colonial knot
centres

Red and apricot
colonial knot
and
lazy daisy
rosebud

Ecru silk
snowdrop

Mustard and
yellow silk
3D daisies

Chain
(green floss
two strand)

Blue silk
forget-me-nots

Green silk
fly stitch

FLAMBOYANT ROSES

BRIDAL BOUQUET

This design is madly "over the top" - It looks stunning as a glamorous cushion tossed onto a Victorian chaise lounge or as a decoration on an exotic jacket.

MATERIALS

Background Cotton
Muslin
Light green embroidery floss
A selection of wide satin ribbon in three shades
Narrow green satin ribbon

INSTRUCTIONS

Lightly pencil the design onto your background fabric. Tack the muslin behind the ground fabric. Begin by embroidering the stems in three strands of light green embroidery thread in *chain stitch* and the leaves in two strands in *romanian*. Now study the methods for making *satin ribbon roses*: (Chapter II Flamboyant roses and large rosebud with calyx, page 19). The large roses are constructed using the *tab method* in the centre, with *trapezoid* petals. Make a *tab method* rosebud and shape the calyx to fit snugly around the bud. Make up a gorgeous cushion cover by adding a border of antique lace and piping, alternatively superimpose the centre design onto moiré taffeta or pure silk.

Bridal bouquet design Bold and beautiful, these roses are constructed using the tab method as the centre with trapezoid petals gathered around this shape. *(Jane Dent)*

Large flamboyant roses

Cabbage rose
tab method

Chain stitch

Romanian leaves

Satin ribbon leaves

Large rosebud with calyx

Satin Pumps Pumps with flamboyant roses are ideal for a bridesmaid or that fancy affair. *(Lesley Turpin-Delport)*

Bridal Bouquet Cushion "A rose by any other name" - utterly feminine for an antique dressing room chair. *(Beryl Soller)*

Page 53

GARDEN HERBS

SAMPLER

Lavender, Camomile, Rosemary, Marjoram, Chives and Dill. Antique doilies, bottle-green background and savoury shades of silk combine in an unusual and quick to make project, ideal for a dining room, patio or breakfast room.

MATERIALS

Six doilies - 14 x 16cm ($5^1/_2$ x $6^1/_4$")
or make your own with white linen and cotton lace.
Silk ribbon: Shades of green, white, yellow, apricot, pastel pink, lilac and lavender
Embroidery thread: Shades of green, yellow, mustard and ecru
Wadding
Bottle-green background fabric

INSTRUCTIONS

Lightly sketch the herbs onto the doilies. Study the labelled drawings and photographs and create your own savoury garden herbs:

Mount the doilies onto bottle-green cotton with wadding under each design for body, and machine stitch in place.

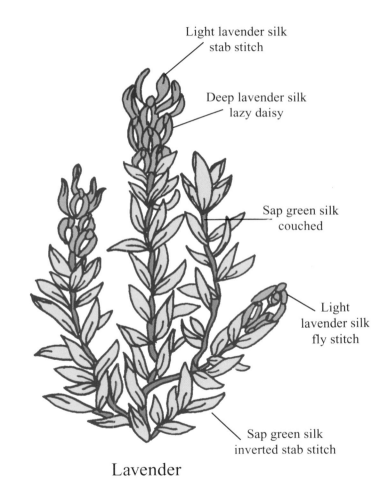

Light lavender silk stab stitch

Deep lavender silk lazy daisy

Sap green silk couched

Light lavender silk fly stitch

Sap green silk inverted stab stitch

Lavender

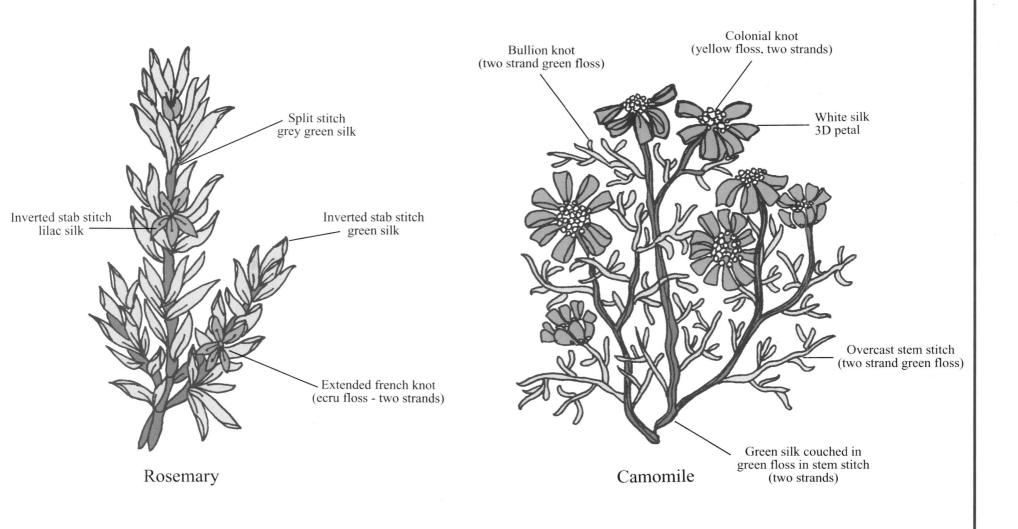

Split stitch
grey green silk

Inverted stab stitch
lilac silk

Inverted stab stitch
green silk

Extended french knot
(ecru floss - two strands)

Rosemary

Bullion knot
(two strand green floss)

Colonial knot
(yellow floss, two strands)

White silk
3D petal

Overcast stem stitch
(two strand green floss)

Green silk couched in
green floss in stem stitch
(two strands)

Camomile

Lavender

Camomile

Rosemary

Marjoram

Chives

Dill

Di Thompson
1993

Garden Herbs

Page 56 – Opposite:
Sampler. Create a sampler of garden herbs in various shades of green silk – lavender, rosemary, camomile, marjoram, chives and dill. *(Di Thomson)*

Parsley. Clusters of fly stitch combine to form a parsley plant. *(Sandra Caister)*

Sage. Applique leaves finished with french knots and pale blue silk blooms completes this botanical plant. *(Sandra Caister)*

Rosemary. No other yarn would work as well as silk ribbon, for a sprig of rosemary. *(Sandra Caister)*

Thyme. The delicacy of the thyme flower is exquisitely rendered in this embroidered herb. *(Sandra Caister)*

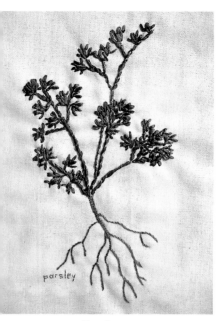

Parsley

Sage

Lavender Blue Tea Cosy. Light and dark lilac and blue silk in romanian stitch is such a simple way of decorating a crisp, white tea cosy. *(Sandra Caister and Anne Neill)*

Rosemary

Thyme

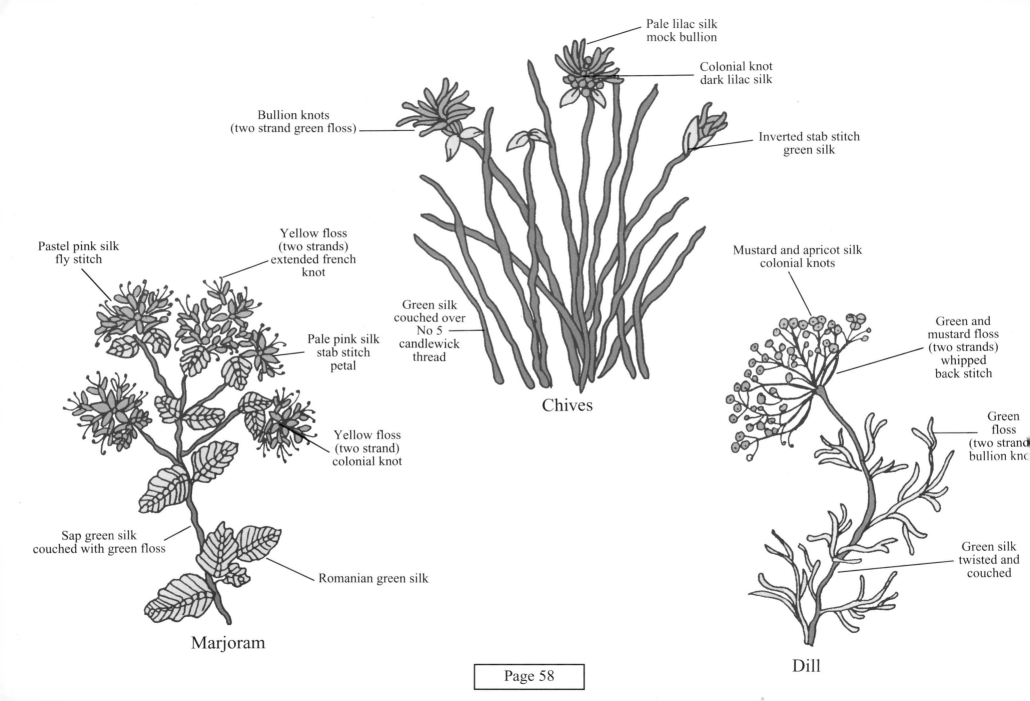

Pale lilac silk
mock bullion

Colonial knot
dark lilac silk

Bullion knots
(two strand green floss)

Inverted stab stitch
green silk

Yellow floss
(two strands)
extended french
knot

Pastel pink silk
fly stitch

Mustard and apricot silk
colonial knots

Pale pink silk
stab stitch
petal

Green and
mustard floss
(two strands)
whipped
back stitch

Green silk
couched over
No 5
candlewick
thread

Green
floss
(two strand
bullion kno

Yellow floss
(two strand)
colonial knot

Chives

Sap green silk
couched with green floss

Green silk
twisted and
couched

Romanian green silk

Marjoram

Dill

Page 58

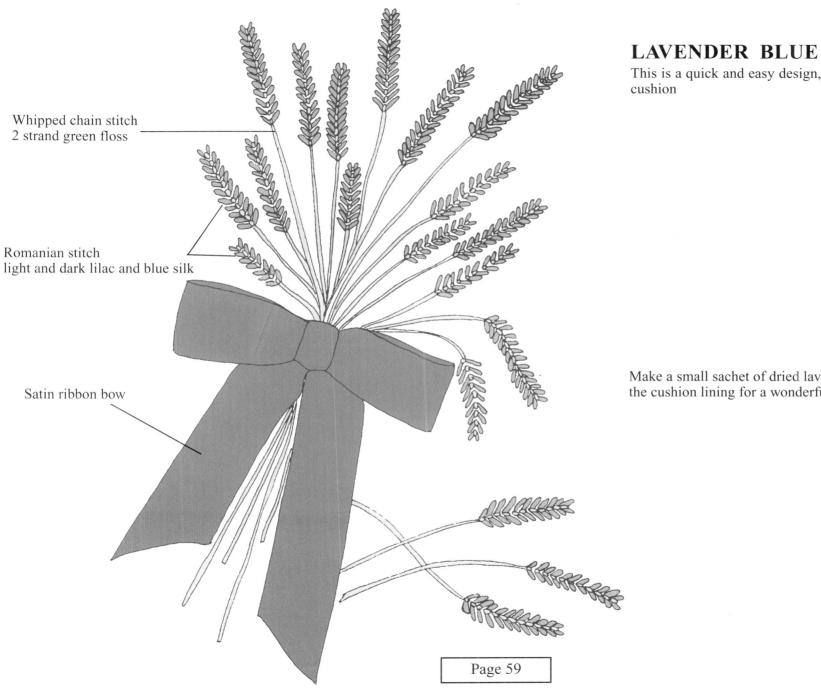

Whipped chain stitch
2 strand green floss

Romanian stitch
light and dark lilac and blue silk

Satin ribbon bow

LAVENDER BLUE
This is a quick and easy design, ideal for a tea cosy or cushion

Make a small sachet of dried lavender and pop it into the cushion lining for a wonderful herbal aroma.

Page 59

SILKEN FEATHERS

Fabric paint and highlights of silk produce an illusion of a silken cockerel

MATERIALS
Biscuit coloured, cotton background fabric.
Muslin
Water based fabric paints: Cherry red, white, black, mustard and grey-green.
Brushes: One stiff bristle brush and one fine, sharp pointed brush.
A selection of silk: Cherry red, white, cinnamon, oyster, black, bottle green, sap green and grey green.

INSTRUCTIONS

Begin by testing your paint on a small piece of scrap fabric to gain a little confidence. Use the paint very diluted, to give the delicate watercolour effect. For easy brush control, mix your paint and water to a creamy consistency. For the dragged feather effect, use the pigment directly from the pot without adding any water. Try different size paint brushes: a fat stiff bristle brush will give a good stipple or drag efect; a medium size, stiff bristle brush is good for the smaller areas and a small fine brush is needed for delicate detail.
Finish off with the fine details, especially the white highlights. Heat seal the paintwork by ironing with a hot iron. Once you have painted the cockerel, tack the muslin behind the background fabric, ready for embroidery.
Study the labelled sketch, photographs and the selection of embroidery stitches and create the ruffled feathers of a silken cockerel.

Detail of the cockerel on opposite page

Silken Feathers

Use sweeping paint strokes under your silk ribbon embroidery for a dramatic effect. Inspired by wildlife artist Charles Tunnicliffe. (*Lesley Turpin-Delport*)

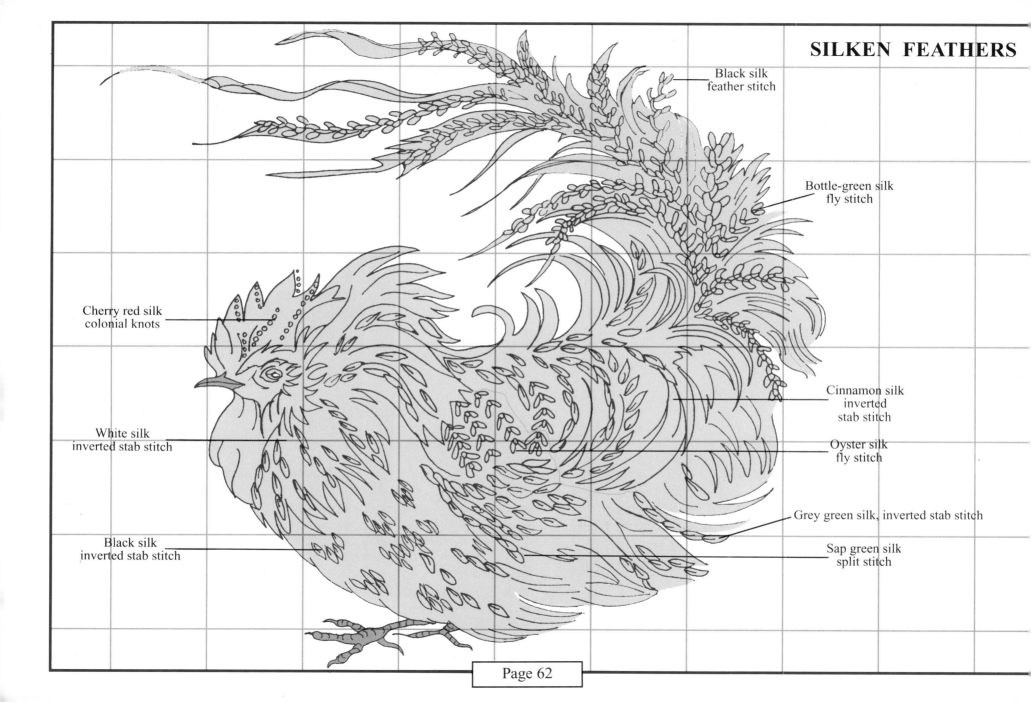

SILKEN FEATHERS

Black silk
feather stitch

Bottle-green silk
fly stitch

Cherry red silk
colonial knots

Cinnamon silk
inverted
stab stitch

White silk
inverted stab stitch

Oyster silk
fly stitch

Grey green silk, inverted stab stitch

Black silk
inverted stab stitch

Sap green silk
split stitch

Page 62

FIGHTING COCKS

Bottle green fly stitch

White silk split stitch

Red silk colonial knot

White silk colonial knot

White silk lazy daisy

Cinnamon silk split stitch

Sap green silk fishbone

Black silk feather stitch

Oyster silk fishbone

Bullions mustard floss (two strands)

White silk inverted stab

White silk colonial knot & black silk lazy daisy

Buttonhole mustard floss (two strands)

Bottle-green fly stitch

Cinnamon silk colonial knot & lazy daisy

Bottle-green silk colonial knots

Bullions mustard floss (two strands)

Mainly pure silk ribbon and clever crewel stitch combinations give texture to an exciting pair of fighting cocks

MATERIALS

White cotton background fabric
Muslin
A selection of silk ribbon: Red, black, white, sap green, bottle green, cinnamon and oyster.
Mustard embroidery floss

INSTRUCTIONS

Enlarge the design to suit your taste and style and lightly pencil the fighting cocks onto your background fabric. Tack the muslin behind the background fabric in preparation for your embroidery.

Study the labelled sketch and photograph on the next page and have fun designing the different feathers. Note that the legs and beaks are in two strands of mustard embroidery floss.

Fighting Cocks

Repetition of simple stitches gives an illusion of the roosters' richly coloured feathers.
(Salli van Rensburg)